CRAYOLA
SUPER EASY
CRAFTS

Rebecca Felix

LERNER PUBLICATIONS ◆ MINNEAPOLIS

The photographs in this book were created by Mighty Media, Inc.

Official Licensed Product
Lerner Publications Company
A division of Lerner Publishing Group, Inc.
241 First Avenue North
Minneapolis, MN 55401 USA

For reading levels and more information, look up this title at www.lernerbooks.com.

Main body text set in Mikado a 14/19.
Typeface provided by HVD Fonts.

Library of Congress Cataloging-in-Publication Data

Names: Felix, Rebecca, 1984– author.
Title: Crayola super easy crafts / by Rebecca Felix.
Description: Minneapolis : Lerner Publications, [2019] | Series: Colorful crayola crafts | Includes bibliographical references and index. | Audience: Ages 9–11. | Audience: Grades 4 to 6.
Identifiers: LCCN 2018002324 (print) | LCCN 2018020412 (ebook) | ISBN 9781541512511 (eb pdf) | ISBN 9781541510999 (lb : alk. paper)
Subjects: LCSH: Handicraft—Juvenile literature. | Science projectsJuvenile literature. | Crayons—Juvenile literature.
Classification: LCC TT160 (ebook) | LCC TT160 .F4575 2019 (print) | DDC 745.5—dc23

LC record available at https://lccn.loc.gov/2018002324

Manufactured in the United States of America
1-43983-33997-9/4/2018

Contents

PAGE PLUS

Scan QR codes throughout for step-by-step photos of each craft.

MAKE SIMPLE PROJECTS IN A SNAP!

Are you a maker? You can be! Follow the steps to create fun, easy crafts.

Let the photos and colorful materials inspire you. Add your own spin to each project for a personal touch. Let's get creative with crafts and color!

Crafting Safety

▶ **Ask adults** for permission to use sharp tools.

▶ **Keep workspaces clean** and free of clutter.

▶ **Work carefully** with paints and glues. Do not touch your face or eyes while using these materials. Wash your hands after use.

Super Easy Tips

▶ Make simple crafts even easier using materials you have on hand!

▬ Swap tape for glue, paint for markers, or notebook paper for construction paper.

▶ Brainstorm ways to combine steps or put a material to new use.

▶ Prepare before a craft to make cleanup super easy.

▬ Cover your workspace with newspaper.

▬ Place a jar or cup of soapy water nearby when painting. Soak used paintbrushes in it right away.

▬ Put tools away immediately after use.

FINGER FIGURINES

Transform just two materials into tiny fingertip puppets!

Materials
- air-dry clay
- water
- newspaper
- paint
- paintbrushes

1 Form clay around your finger to make a puppet body.

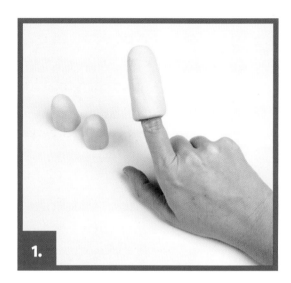

1.

2. Remove the clay body from your finger. Add a clay head, arms, ears, nose, and any other features to your puppet. Be careful not to crush the body as you work. Add some water to the clay where body parts attach. This helps the clay pieces stick together.

2.

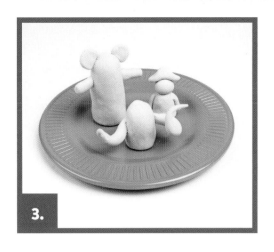

3.

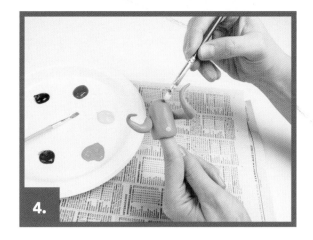

4.

3. Repeat steps 1 through 2 to make more puppets. Let the clay dry overnight.

4. Cover your work surface in newspaper. Paint your puppets. When the paint dries, your tiny characters are ready to wear!

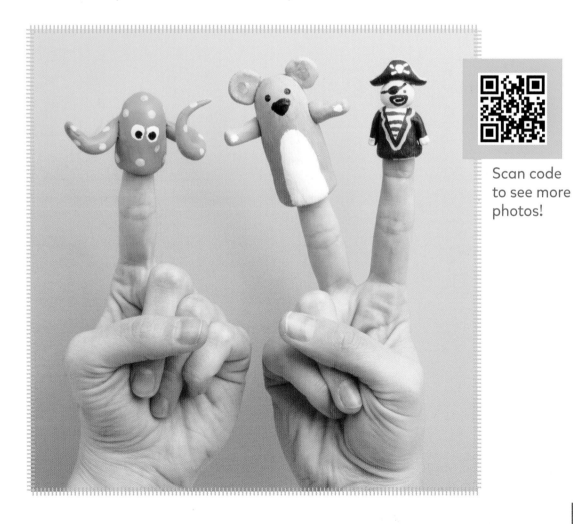

Scan code to see more photos!

PATTERNED PENCIL SPINNERS

Use paper shapes to turn a pencil into a spinning work of art!

Materials
- pencils
- small box
- cup
- card stock
- scissors
- markers
- glitter glue

1. Trace the small box and the top of the cup on card stock. Cut out the shapes.

2. Decorate one side of each shape with markers and glitter glue. Symmetrical designs look best when spinning!

2.

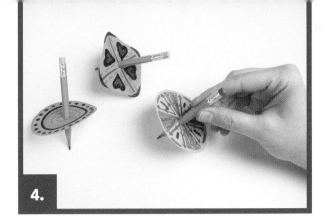

3. Once the glue is dry, ask an adult to help you carefully punch a sharpened pencil through the decorated side of each shape.

4. Spin the pencils on their sharpened ends. Watch your colorful designs swirl!

Tip!
Shorter pencils work best as spinners. They balance better because they have a lower center of gravity.

BITTY BRICKS

Design little bricks in four simple steps. Then use them to build endless structures!

Materials
- air-dry clay
- silicone baking mold
- water
- plastic knife
- sponge
- paint
- paintbrushes

1.

1. Press and form bricks of clay in the molds. Use water to keep the clay soft and workable.

2. Use a plastic knife to smooth and level the tops of the bricks.

3. Use a wet sponge to clean the tray and smooth the bricks even more.

2.

4. Let the clay dry overnight.

5. Paint the bricks. When the paint dries, use them to construct bridges, buildings, and more!

Tip!
If your silicone mold is too floppy to form bricks easily, try using an ice cube tray instead!

WOVEN WATERCOLORS

Paint, weave, and frame a unique work of art!

Materials

- newspaper
- water color paint
- water
- paintbrushes
- paper
- scissors
- glue stick
- construction paper

1. Cover your work surface in newspaper. Paint two sheets of paper with colorful designs. Contrasting colors will create a bold look when woven!

2. Once the paint is dry, cut one sheet of paper in horizontal strips. Discard one strip.

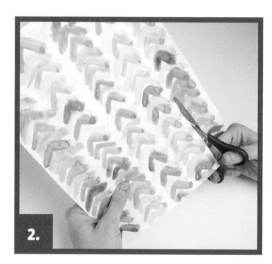

2.

3. Fold the second sheet of paper in half the long way. Cut vertical slits into it, stopping 1 inch (2.5 cm) from the edge. Unfold the paper carefully.

3.

4. Lay the long strips horizontally. Weave the short strips through them. Go under then over every other strip. Rub glue where the strips meet.

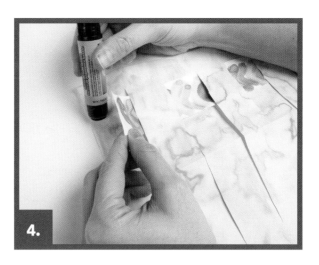

5. Glue the woven sheets onto construction paper as a frame. Then display your watercolor work of art!

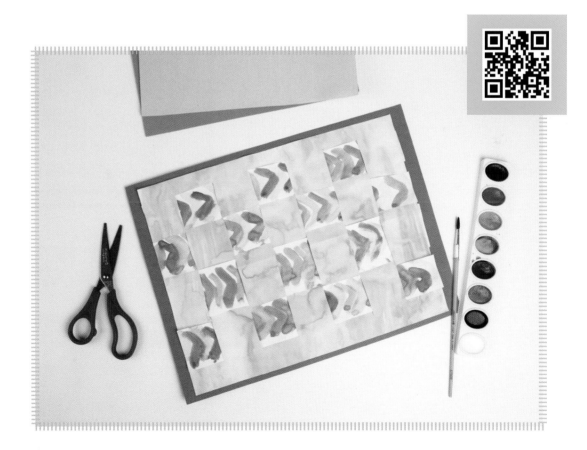

EASY EMOJI PINS

Make colorful, cute pins in minutes!

Materials

- school glue
- flat plastic lid or plastic folder
- fine line black marker
- paint
- paintbrushes
- adhesive glue dots
- safety pins

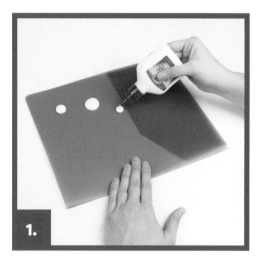

1. Squeeze one circular blob of glue onto the lid or folder for each pin you want to make. Let the glue dry for one to two nights.

2. Peel the blobs from the plastic.

3. Draw emoji expressions on the flat back side of each blob.

4. Paint over the faces with a solid color. Let the paint dry.

5. Place a glue dot on the painted side of each blob. This is to hold the safety pin upright. Place the closed side of an open safety pin on each glue dot. Then cover the dot in glue.

6. When the glue dries, attach your pins to a jacket, backpack, and more!

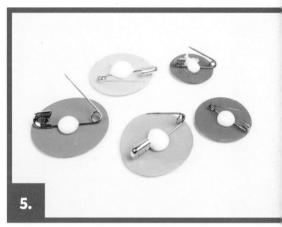

4.

5.

HOMEMADE MANDALA MURAL

Draw and design bright discs to create a colorful wall display.

Materials
- pencil
- plastic plate or bowl larger than a CD or DVD disc
- fine line markers
- paper
- CD or DVD disc
- ruler
- scissors
- tape

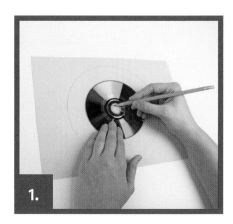
1.

1. Trace the bowl or plate on the paper. Center the disc in the traced circle. Trace the disc's outer rim and inner circle.

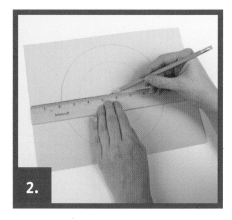
2.

2. Use a ruler to draw a vertical and horizontal line across the circles. These will be guidelines.

3.

3. Draw a shape in the center of the smallest circle. Draw a row of shapes around the first shape. Continue until the small circle is full of shapes.

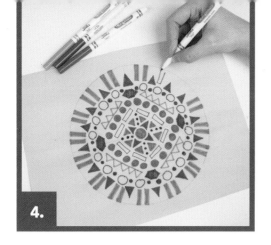

4. Draw circular rows of shapes until the other circle is filled as well. Alternate outline colors, and color in some shapes.

5. Cut out the largest circle. You've made a mandala!

6. Repeat steps 1 through 5 to make more mandalas. Tape them together to make a mural.

COFFEE FILTER FLOWERS

Make coffee filters bloom into beautiful flowers.

Materials
- coffee filters
- paper clips
- markers
- plastic plate
- paper towels
- water
- scissors
- twist ties
- chenille stems (pipe cleaners)

1. Use one coffee filter for each flower you want to make. Fold each filter in half three times to make a triangle shape. Clip the folds in place.

2 Color one side of the filters. It's okay if there are some white spaces.

3. Set the filters on the plate. Place a folded, wet paper towel on top of each filter. Let the paper towels sit for five minutes, and then remove them. Let the filters dry overnight.

4. Trim the rounded side of each triangle so the filter looks like a petal.

5. Remove the paper clips, and unfold the filters. Pinch together each flower's center, and wrap a twist tie around it.

6. Wrap a chenille stem around each twist tie to make a flower stem. Gently shape and open the filter to look like a flower. Display your bouquet in a cup, vase, or pencil holder!

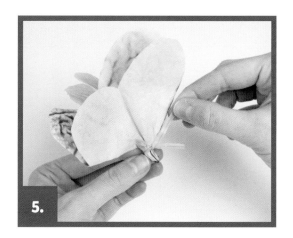

CARDBOARD AND CLAY CHECKERS

Craft cardboard and clay into a colorful board game.

Materials

- scissors
- cardboard cereal box
- ruler
- pencil
- newspaper
- paint
- plastic plate
- sponge
- clay
- paintbrushes

1. Cut the cardboard box along one long edge to open it into a large rectangle. Measure and draw a large square on the cardboard. Cut out the shape.

2. Cover your work surface in newspaper, and paint the square. Let the paint dry.

3. Measure one edge of the square. Divide this measurement by eight. This number will be the size of each square. Measure and cut the sponge to this size. Dip the sponge piece in paint, and stamp it along one edge of the square four times. Start in the corner and space the stamps evenly.

4. Stamp another row, but start it under the first open space in the row above. Repeat six times to make eight rows total. Let the paint dry.

5. Form 24 clay balls. Flatten and shape them slightly to make round discs. Let the clay dry overnight.

6. Paint 12 discs a bright color. Leave the others white, or paint them another color. When the paint dries, use these pieces to play checkers on your new board!

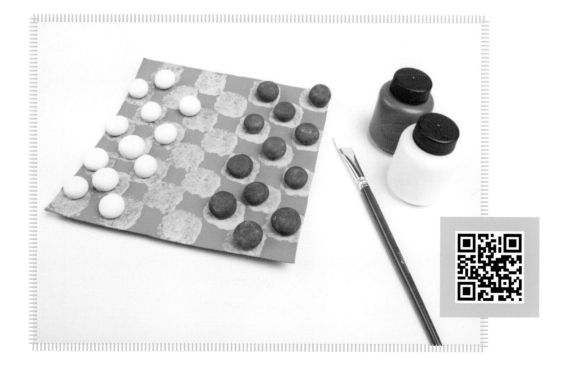

THREE-STEP BEADS

Build small beads from clay, and create cool accessories.

Materials
- air-dry clay
- small paintbrushes
- paint
- newspaper
- plastic plates
- string or ribbon
- scissors
- 2 small, low-power magnets
- school glue

1. Form several small beads from clay. Gently push the end of a small paintbrush through each ball to make a hole through its center. Smooth the hole openings as needed. Let the clay dry overnight.

1.

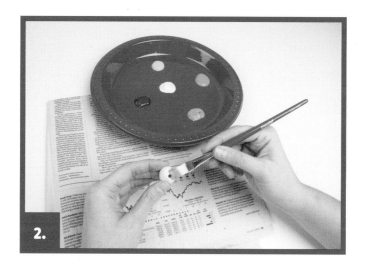

2. Cover your work surface in newspaper, and put paint on a plastic plate. Paint the beads, and let them dry.

3. Thread the beads onto string or ribbon. Glue one magnet to each ribbon end. Let the glue dry. Then connect these magnets to wear the necklace!

WEARABLE ART

Design and dye your own apparel using markers and glue!

Materials

- fabric markers
- spray bottles
- water
- scissors
- cardboard
- light-colored, plain cotton clothing
- paper
- marker
- school glue
- large garbage bag
- plastic plate
- washer
- dryer

1. For each color of marker you want to use, fill one spray bottle with a bit of water.

2. Remove the caps from the markers. Place one marker inside each bottle so the marker tips are underwater. Let the bottles sit overnight. The marker ink will bleed into the water.

2.

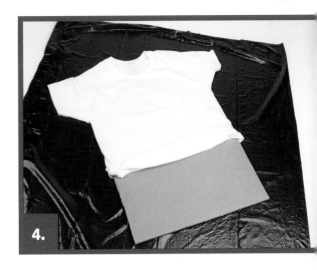

3. Cut a piece of cardboard to fit inside the clothing item, and create a flat surface on it.

4. Place the clothing item on the large garbage bag to protect your work surface.

5. Draw a design on a piece of paper for practice.

Tip!
The less water in a spray bottle, the darker the color's shade will be on the shirt. More water will create lighter shades.

Wearable Art
continued next page

6. Draw the design on the clothing in glue. Allow the glue to dry overnight.

7. Remove the cardboard, and lay the clothing item flat again on the plastic bag.

8. Remove the markers from the spray bottles. Set the markers on a plastic plate to dry out.

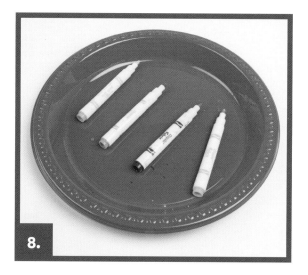

9. Reattach the spray nozzles to each bottle.

10. Spray the clothing item with the dyed water. Spray until the item is soaked through with dye.

11. Allow the dye to dry overnight. Then have an adult help you put the clothing item in the dryer for 30 minutes. This sets the dye. Wash the item in the washing machine. The glue will wash away, and you will be left with a cool, dyed clothing masterpiece!

10.

Tip!
Save old clothes and use them to create other costumes.

Get Creative!

Look at materials, steps, and craft photos. Are you missing some materials to re-create a craft? Would you have done the craft differently? Try it out!

Find new ways to make each project your own. Try swapping tissue paper for coffee filters or paint for markers. Make square mandalas or clay figurines that fit your whole hand! With art supplies and some imagination, the possibilities are endless.

Glossary

alternate: to arrange by every other color, shape, or other factor

horizontal: straight and level from side to side

inspire: to encourage or influence to achieve, do, or make something

mandala: a graphic pattern usually in the form of a circle divided into sections or having multiple circular rows of shapes and images

mural: a large painting or work of art on a wall

permission: agreement to allow something to happen

symmetrical: having matching points, parts, or shapes on both sides of a dividing line

transform: to completely change something

unique: unlike anything else

vertical: straight up and down

To Learn More

Books

Bernhardt, Carolyn. *Duct Tape Fashion*. Minneapolis: Lerner Publications, 2017.
Create cool costumes from colorful duct tape. Tips and duct tape facts will help make you a master crafter!

Dorobek, Jamie. *C.R.A.F.T.: Creating Really Awesome Free Things; 100 Seriously Fun, Super-Easy Projects for Kids*. Avon, MA: Adams Media, 2016.
Transform items you have at home into cool crafts! Find photos and step-by-step directions for making 100 different creations.

Gonzalez-Pell, Cintia. *Make in a Day: Crafts for Kids*. Mineola, NY: Dover Publications, 2018.
Make simple crafts with everyday supplies! Each beginner-level project can be begun and completed in one day.

Websites

Burst of Color Tracings
http://www.crayola.com/crafts/burst-of-color-tracings-craft/
Gather items at home and trace them onto paper. Color in the shapes to make easy abstract artwork!

Crafts for Kids
http://www.pbs.org/parents/crafts-for-kids/
Discover a huge list of kid-friendly crafts!

Kids Crafts and Activities
http://www.hellokids.com/r_401/kids-crafts-and-activities
Follow simple step-by-step instructions to make all sorts of cool crafts. Some even have printable templates!

Index